T0209450

It's NOT *for* SALE

KARL A. GROSVENOR

WESTBOW
P R E S S®
A DIVISION OF THOMAS NELSON
& ZONDERVAN

WestBow Press books may be ordered through booksellers or by contacting:

WestBow Press
A Division of Thomas Nelson & Zondervan
1663 Liberty Drive
Bloomington, IN 47403
www.westbowpress.com
1 (866) 928-1240

ISBN: 978-1-9736-3569-7 (sc)
ISBN: 978-1-9736-3570-3 (e)

Library of Congress Control Number: 2018909074

Print information available on the last page.

WestBow Press rev. date: 08/09/2018

To the memory of my mother and father,
Evelyn and Elliott Grosvenor,
who taught me love and honesty.

To the memory of my mother-in–law and father-in-law,
Amelia and Ernest Gittens,
who took me into their family because of love and honesty.

To the memory of my sister Doriel,
who was a spiritual example and mentor to us
in the absence of our father and mother.

To the memory of my sister Beulah Sahadath,
who entrusted me with the responsibility
of her only son, Dave Sahadath.

To the memory of my brother-in-law, John Gittens, who in
1989 exemplified my original idea of live, love, and laugh.

Contents

Foreword.. ix

Preface xi

Acknowledgments xiii

Introduction..xv

Chapter 1   The Offer 1

Chapter 2   The Contract..18

Chapter 3   The Signature: The Writing on the Wall ... 29

Chapter 4   Historic Roots of Sacrifice......................... 40

Chapter 5   Money Matters 56

Chapter 6   The End Time.. 63

Chapter 7   Televangelists and the Tithe...................... 71

Chapter 8   News Flash! 79

About the Author.. 85

Foreword

My name is Sharon Grosvenor. I am a registered nurse. My bachelor of science in nursing and master of arts in business administration have eminently qualified me for my position as assistant director of nursing at the largest hospital in Brooklyn, New York, where I have worked for many years.

I am extremely proud to have met the author of this book, Karl Grosvenor, on a Sunday night after a church service, where he preached a sermon entitled "After All This, Then What?" This meeting led to the best thing that ever happened to me: he asked for my hand in marriage, to which I immediately replied, "*Yes*." Thank you, Karl, for the portion of your acknowledgment which states, "I wish to express my sincere gratitude to my dear wife Sharon Rose, who has been the driving force behind my decision to write this book, for her encouragement and dedication in helping me with its completion."

Karl Grosvenor holds a bachelor's degree in business administration and has a vast amount of knowledge in church dealings. He was very active in his church work as an authorized preacher, vice president of the young people's society, and member of the church choir. He once collaborated with his president to organize an all-night prayer meeting. He wrote and, with his president, directed a play for the church's zone meetings. He has delivered countless sermons to church congregations.

In this book, he paints a vivid picture of the church and the way it has grown from its grassroots stage to a massive organization, its beliefs and teachings about tithing, its businesslike operating methods, and the manner in which it obtains its financial support. While his intent is not to sway anyone from personal belief or to cast a negative light on any religious organization, the hope is that this book will help readers understand why he believes that some evangelists today have misrepresented and continue to misrepresent the meaning of tithing and its purpose, while enriching themselves with fancy cars, jets, and multimillion-dollar homes.

Preface

I have had the privilege of shopping at many retail establishments, seeking an item of quality, yet priced at an affordable level that would allow me to make a purchase.

Very often, items are advertised as being "on sale." Some businesses, for example in the pharmaceutical industry, advertise these items to influence customers to try the products. However, when we read the labels, we would find the words *"Not for sale."*

Acknowledgments

I would like to express my deepest appreciation and indebtedness to all my relatives, friends, and others who, in one way or another, shared their support in the completion of this book.

I wish to express my sincere gratitude to my dear wife Sharon Rose, who has been the driving force behind my decision to write this book, for her encouragement and dedication in helping me with its completion.

Above all, thanks to God Almighty for His help and strength, and to my Lord and Savior Jesus Christ, who paid for our sins with His blood.

Introduction

The way we view religion today has changed immensely from past perspectives. The introduction and accessibility of technology have led to a businesslike presentation of evangelism to the masses. Competition is strong among grassroots churches, which vie for larger buildings in order to accommodate their expanding congregations. Money has become an important factor in the expansion of these organizations. The way in which money is obtained has become questionable.

CHAPTER 1

THE OFFER

Buy the truth, and sell *it* not; *als*o wisdom,
and instruction, and understanding.

—Proverbs 23:23

In the early Old Testament days, the Israelites had no currency. Therefore, trading was done by the barter system, which involved numbers, weights, and measurements. The world's economies today operate on a similar system. This system involves trading or buying and selling commodities, whether they are stocks and bonds, real estate, motor vehicles, equipment, food, and so on. Everything has a price. To make the sale final, there must be an offer and an acceptance. This scenario is known as a contract.

The ordinary person buys products for personal use. However, some people are in the business of buying and selling for the sole purpose of financial gain—in other words, to become rich. Wealth becomes an obsession, and some will spare no effort to obtain it. There are numerous commodities that can and will be offered for sale; likewise, whatever is offered for sale can be and will be bought.

But can the truth be treated as a commodity and offered for sale, and if so, at what price? Can anyone determine the monetary value, and can anyone really *buy or sell the truth*?

The NIV Rainbow Study Bible has translated the above passage of Scripture to read, "Buy the truth and do not sell it." Since the word "buy" denotes some sort of monetary exchange, again we ask, can a value be placed upon the truth? If so, who owns the truth, and who can or will determine the value? Can the truth really be bought or sold? Will it be sold to the highest bidder?

Before we get into the discussion about the value of truth, we need to determine what truth is. If we revert to the first act or offer of sale, we can reflect on the situation that existed in the garden of Eden. The serpent approached Eve and offered her the opportunity to acquire the position of a god with the knowledge of good and evil. The serpent said humanity would gain this knowledge by eating the fruit God had forbidden them to eat.

When God placed Adam and Eve in the garden of Eden, He gave them dominion over everything except the fruit of the tree of life. God gave them strict instructions: "The day that thou eatest of this tree, thou shalt surely die."

This is where the tradeoff came in. The devil took the opportunity to gain points with Eve by making God out to be a liar or, as we would say, a stranger to the truth. Cunningly, the devil said to Eve, "Ye shall not surely die: For God doth know that in the day ye eat thereof, then your eyes shall be opened, and ye shall be as gods knowing good and evil."

The acquisition of knowledge and the ability to discern between good and evil, along with the possibility of living forever, was too good an offer for Eve to refuse. The offer was accepted, and the sale was completed. The devil gained the confidence of two people with whom God had a very close relationship, and they sold their souls for what they thought was a great gain.

While the previous scenario has absolutely nothing to do with financial gain, it has everything to do with the willingness of people to gain an advantage in whatever manner they can. Today we are faced with the same situation as Eve. We are being offered the opportunity to obtain knowledge through a company that bears the name of the fruit: Apple. This apple was not grown on a tree. It is a company that was the brainchild of a gentleman who devoted his life to the quest for knowledge. Is it a coincidence that the diagram of the apple on the cover of its devices has a piece bitten out as if it is being eaten? Was the company's founder inspired by Eve's ready acceptance of the devil's cloaked offer? What price did the founder pay for his knowledge? We do not know. But we do know that the price we are being asked to pay for the knowledge provided through his company continues to grow higher and higher.

There is absolutely nothing wrong with anyone having a desire to be wealthy once one's emotions are not driven by that desire.

There are many people mentioned in the Bible who were rich. Some were rich because of physical commodities, such as farmland, sheep, camels, and trade goods. Some became rich because of their faithfulness to God, and thus were blessed in the sense that their material worth was increased severalfold. There were also those who sought to become rich by robbing others. Those were the people whom Jesus, in anger, whipped and cast out of the temple. Their only concern at that stage was financial. Maybe they were trying to sell a distorted truth.

In the Bible, we read of that instance when wealth took preeminence over worship: "And Jesus went into the temple of God and cast out all them that sold and bought in the temple and overthrew the tables of the money changers and the seats of them that sold doves. And said unto them, 'It is written. My house shall be called the house of prayer; but ye have made it a den of thieves'" (Matt. 21:12-13 KJV).

The anger displayed by Jesus when He drove them out of the temple was not because the merchants sold commodities and changed money. He was aware of the business factor since His disciples were involved in all sorts of businesses. The problem was that these people were using the temple as a marketplace for conducting business rather than as a place of worship.

Jesus was no stranger to the significance of contracts. In the business world, a contract cannot be binding if the person to whom the offer is made is of unsound mind, is a minor, or refuses or fails to accept the terms of the offer. After His baptism, Jesus experienced His first temptation in the form of a trade offer. There were several suggestions made to influence the trade, but there was one offer made based upon His physical condition and His mental strain. He had fasted for forty days and nights. Therefore, we can well imagine how hunger would have made it easy for Him to succumb to the offer. Satan suggested that Jesus use His heavenly authority to create food from the very stones to satisfy His human need. However, Jesus refused to allow His physical condition to overpower His spiritual strength and rejected the offer.

Proposal after proposal was presented without success. Finally, the devil thought up a plan that he believed would capture the imagination of Jesus, an offer above all offers and one that any earthly person could not refuse. The devil ignored the fact that Jesus was the heir to the throne of the King of Kings and Lord of Lords, and offered Him the wealth of the world. However, there was a catch to this offer. The required exchange was almost like embarking on an illegal trade. Therefore, there could be no acceptance.

In other words, the devil was trying to trade the things that he thought would be of great significance to the earthly aspect of Jesus. Satan showed Jesus all the kingdoms of the world and the glory of them, and offered them in exchange for Jesus's personal worship of Satan. But Jesus knew that there was no lasting earthly glory to the things being offered, and that His worship and service should be to His heavenly Father. They were not for sale or barter.

In the Bible is another recorded transaction involving an offer and acceptance. Although this transaction did not evolve from the offer for sale of a marketable commodity, it nevertheless played upon the susceptibility of the human nature and the pangs of hunger.

The story is found in chapter 25 of the book of Genesis. It concerns twin brothers, Jacob and Esau. Esau, being the firstborn, was heir to the wealth of his father. Esau was a hunter. He came home from the fields famished and was willing to give anything for a meal.

Jacob, who was a simple man and lived in a tent, was preparing a pot of soup. Esau requested some. Jacob, realizing his brother's psychological weakness due to hunger, seized the opportunity to acquire something that, to his mind, was of greater value than his soup. At this point, Jacob suddenly became a shrewd businessman. He said to Esau, "Sell me this day thy birthright," and offered his brother a bowl of soup in exchange.

Esau realized that life was more important than anything his brother asked in exchange. His reasoning was that the birthright was of no value to him if he died from hunger. So he was willing to relinquish his birthright for a bowl of soup.

Jacob required no signature or witness. All he needed was acceptance of his offer. He grasped the opportunity and gave Esau a meal in exchange for the birthright.

Another case in the book of Genesis is that of Abraham, whose name was Abram before he journeyed to Egypt. Because of his obedience to God, God rewarded him by making him the father of many nations. However, this was only spiritual wealth. Abraham's material wealth was not acquired through his obedience to God, but rather because of his deception with intent to save his own life. To do this, he said that his wife Sarai was his sister. Abraham did stretch the truth a bit because Sarai was really his half-sister. Abraham was treated well by Pharaoh and became the recipient of great wealth. He was very rich in cattle, silver, and gold, but his wealth never got in the way of his belief and faith in God. Therefore, God added to his wealth by providing him a large quantity of land.

Job was another rich man mentioned in the Bible. The first chapter of the book of Job states that Job was perfect and upright, and one who feared God and avoided evil. Why did Job receive such a blessing from God? Nothing is mentioned about his financial dealings or about the tithes he paid or sacrifices he made, only that he was perfect and upright and avoided evil.

Job never allowed his wealth to get in the way of his faith and respect for God. He often assembled his family for worship and ensured that God was first and foremost in his life. His friends ridiculed him, and because of his trials and discomfort, his wife also turned on him and suggested that he curse God and die. Job's wealth was not his problem; his friends were his problem.

Satan challenged God, suggesting that Job's wealth was the reason Job remained so faithful. God knew Job's faithfulness and gave Satan the authority to afflict Job in any way Satan desired, with one exception: Job's life was off limits.

Solomon, the richest king in the Bible, obtained his wealth because of his honesty and humility. He realized how inadequate he was and that he was incapable of judging the people over whom he was placed to rule. He asked God for wisdom. There was no pretense; Solomon knew his limitations. Despite his inherited wealth, no amount of money could buy knowledge and understanding. God gave him what he had asked for and more. We read that kings and queens from all over the world sought Solomon's wisdom and brought him gifts of gold, silver, and jewels.

> In Gibeon the Lord appeared to Solomon in a dream by night: and God said, "Ask what I shall give thee."

> And Solomon said, "Thou hast shewed unto thy servant David my father great mercy, according as he walked before thee in truth, and in righteousness, and in uprightness of heart with thee; and thou hast kept for him this great kindness, that thou hast given him a son to sit on his throne, as it is this day."

> And now, O Lord my God, thou hast made thy servant king instead of David my father: and I am but a little child: I know not how to go out or come in.

> And thy servant is in the midst of thy people which thou hast chosen, a great people,

that cannot be numbered nor counted for multitude.

Give therefore thy servant an understanding heart to judge thy people that I may discern between good and bad: for who is able to judge this thy so great a people?

And the speech pleased the Lord, that Solomon had asked this thing.

And God said unto him, because thou hast asked this thing, and hast not asked for thyself long life; neither hast asked riches for thyself, nor hast asked the life of thy enemies; but hast asked for thyself understanding to discern judgment.

Behold I have done according to thy words: lo I have given thee a wise and an understanding heart; so that there was none like thee before thee, neither after thee shall any arise like unto thee.

And I have also given thee that which thou hast not asked, both riches and honour: so that there shall not be any among the kings like unto thee all thy days.

And if thou wilt walk in my ways, to keep my statutes and my commandments, as thy

father David did walk, then I will lengthen
thy days. (1 Kings 3:5–14 KJV)

Perhaps Solomon knew that, having succeeded to his father's
throne, he would inherit wealth, but wisdom is the principal
thing. Wisdom cannot be inherited; it would have to be
obtained as a direct gift from God. Therefore, Solomon
chose to ask God for wisdom.

There was also a condition to this gift. Solomon was required
to walk in God's ways and keep God's statutes, as his father
David had done. In return, God promised to lengthen his
days.

Solomon knew that wisdom was essential. Without it, he
would be unable to manage his wealth, which in turn could
be fleeting. "Wilt thou set thine eyes upon that which is not?
For riches certainly make themselves wings; they fly away as
an eagle toward heaven" (Prov. 23:5 KJV).

Everyone cannot be an Abraham, a Jacob, a Job, or a
Solomon, but we can all use their lives, successes, and failures
as examples whereby we can set our spiritual compasses.

Remember we spoke before of early civilization in which
the words "buy" and "sell" were not used. They spoke of
"barter," which means a swap or equal exchange. No money
was involved. They simply exchanged items that they agreed
were of equal value, e.g., fifty sheep for a camel or thirty
sheep for twenty bags of corn. Barter proved to be very
lucrative for those who had the property to trade.

There was a sale mentioned in the Bible that was made not for wealth but because of jealousy. Joseph's brothers sold him to the Ishmaelites because he was their father's favorite. Their decision to sell their brother was not for financial gain but to acquire more of their father's love and attention. There is a similarity between the act of Joseph's brothers and that of Judas. Neither of the sellers bargained for what they wanted; in both cases they accepted what they were offered.

In our current system of commerce, where money is the principal factor, buying and selling can prove very lucrative to those who have merchandise to sell. There is a market for everything from toothpicks to TVs. Marketplaces are usually centralized within a city or town. There are also door-to-door salespersons who try to influence people to purchase their products.

Markets have recently expanded from brick-and-mortar settings to ACH (automatic check handling), internet transactions, and telemarketing. The internet, TV, newspapers, and radio are prime means of advertisement. Sales pitches include discounts such as coupons and "buy one and get one free" offers. Some businesses even go as far as posting misleading advertisements, using statements such as "going out for business" instead of "going out of business." The average person never scrutinizes signs; we see what appears to be familiar and assume we understand.

There is a television in almost every home. Every program breaks for commercials about six times per hour, and there are about five commercials per break. The world is a vast marketplace, and whatever can be sold will be bought.

Whatever can be bought has a value. The main objective of all businesses is to amass profit.

There is another type of business (although they say it is "not for profit") that has changed the course of its operations. Once upon a time, evangelism was conducted from a village mission hall. The congregation was not very large. It included small family groups who were members of the church, and the occasional visitors. Sometimes the pastor lived close by, and sometimes he traveled to more than one mission in an area. He led a very simple life. He walked to the church and knew each member by name. The congregation sang such well-known hymns as the one recorded by Burl Ives, "Oh Come, Come, Come to the Church in the Wild Wood." The church bells rang on Sunday mornings, calling people to worship.

Amazingly, that has all changed now. We now speak of towns and cities, not villages. The pastor no longer lives nearby and requires transportation to reach the church. The operation of the church is no longer a one-man show: there is a church board, an assistant to the pastor, deacons, elders, a choir, and ushers. Some pastors broadcast their church services over the radio, television, and internet—an outreach program that also serves as a form of advertisement. As a result, some churches' memberships have grown immensely. What does this really mean?

Some churches have changed their policies about membership. They have implemented activities and programs to capture the imagination of the youth. They have stressed a "come as you are" approach that allows people to attend services in whatever attire they wish. They have replaced a lone organ or piano with bands and allow the practice of line dancing. They advertise their services and offer prayers for those with problems. They ask people to become partners with them for the furtherance of the gospel. It has now become difficult to distinguish what is spiritual from what is secular.

All churches, regardless of denomination, have ordinances or rules that must be adhered to by the members. Some denominations once forbade their members from frequenting movie houses, dance halls or clubs; consuming alcoholic beverages; or being involved in any form of promiscuity. Churches recommended that attire should reflect a Christlike spirit. However, in recent years, most of these standards have changed. Female members are wearing the latest fashions, including pantsuits, and men too wear the hottest styles, regardless of the cost. A glass of wine at dinner is also now acceptable.

In the gospel of John, Jesus prayed to His Father on behalf of His disciples, He asked that they not be taken out of the world, but that they should be kept in the world (John 17:16–17). On the other hand, Jesus stressed the fact that His disciples should not be of the world, as He is not of the world. He prayed for their sanctification. While I am not criticizing some congregations' new methods of operation, I am curious about the reasons for these changes.

Ministers now are acquiring football stadiums in which to conduct their services. The church has gone the way of commerce. Telemarketing has become a huge part of operations. Like the secular world, churches are using television as a means of acquiring a larger market share. They use inspirational speaking and preaching to encourage the audience to accept Christ into their lives, hoping audience members will become members of their organization and regular financial contributors.

There is absolutely nothing wrong with televangelism, other than the fact that religious radio stations have become almost obsolete. Although advancement has always been the objective, I cannot help but think about my youth, when there was no television. My family listened to the radio for everything from news to entertainment. Ministers relied upon member donations to keep their programs on the air; they never sought donations from listeners. Maybe there was no sustainability in their system. This speaks to the wisdom expressed in Ecclesiastes 7:10: "Say not thou, what is the cause that the former days were better than these? For thou hast not enquired wisely concerning this."

The larger the membership grows, the larger the goodwill offerings and donations become. Many of these denominations now advertise as ministries, associations, and organizations, inviting listeners to become partners and describing themselves as "interdenominational." Televangelists own summer and winter homes, luxury cars, yachts, and private jets, acquired perhaps through their personal wealth, perhaps through the wealth of the church. Televangelism has become a very lucrative business.

The important question is, what are the televangelists selling to acquire this wealth? They sell books, tickets for banquets, tickets for cruises, tickets to conventions, and tickets to special programs. They travel to foreign countries to run crusades, which are often paid for by the ministries of the host countries. They leave with a bundle of money from collected offerings. Like secular businesspeople, they try to influence viewers to make donations by offering "free" gifts such as books and CDs of sermons in exchange for financial support. Sermons may be offered for sale outright. Sometimes televangelists record sermons that center on a theme, and as a result are lengthy. A series is required to exhaust the theme. Anyone wanting to acquire the entire sermon must purchase the entire series.

No one can attend a service and excuse themselves from participating in the offertory by saying, "I do not have any money on me." There are now ATMs in the lobbies of some churches, and the ATMs do not dispense small change. You can also make offerings by check or credit card. You can purchase books and CDs in the lobby right after the service.

Are the televangelists only selling books and CDs? It seems that the greatest commodity they have for sale is the *truth*. This brings us back to Matthew 21:12.

However, before I go in depth on this subject, I must define "truth, wisdom and understanding" as stated in the book of Proverbs: "Buy the truth, and sell *it* not; *als*o wisdom, and instruction, and understanding."

The *Merriam-Webster Dictionary* defines "truth" as honesty, fact, actuality, and correctness. "Wisdom" is defined as accumulated philosophic or scientific learning, knowledge, insight, good sense, judgment, or a wise attitude or course of action. "Understanding" is defined as knowledge and ability to judge, agreement of opinion or feeling, or an agreement informally or tactfully entered.

Another dictionary defines "truth" as conformity to fact or actuality, or faithfulness to an original or to a standard. "Wisdom" is defined as the ability to judge correctly and to follow the best course of action based on knowledge and understanding.

In the Old and New Testaments, truth is a fundamental and moral quality of God. God is truth, the Spirit is truth, and Jesus is truth.

In the gospel of John, Jesus told His disciples that He was going to prepare a place for them. He promised that He would come again and take them with Him. Where He would be, there they would be also. He said that they knew the way to the place where He would be going.

Thomas confessed to Jesus that he did not know the way. Jesus responded, "I am the way and the truth and the life, no man cometh to the Father but by Me" (John 14:6).

If God is truth, the Spirit is truth, and Jesus is the way, the truth, and the life, can Proverbs 23:23 be ignored? Should we be willing to exploit the truth for financial gain?

> In the beginning was the Word and the Word was with God and the Word was God. (John 1:1)

> And the Word was made flesh and dwelt among us. (And we beheld his glory, the glory as of the only begotten of the Father.) Full of grace and truth. (John 1:14)

Televangelists are not the only ones trying to sell the truth. There is record of a transaction that took place in the New Testament involving the truth. Anytime there is an offer of payment for any kind of service, action, or commodity, it constitutes an offer, which triggers the possibility of an acceptance or a meeting of the minds. Once an offer is accepted, the agreement becomes a contract.

CHAPTER 2

THE CONTRACT

The chief priests, scribes, and elders of the people assembled in the palace of the high priest Caiaphas to formulate a plan to secretly capture and kill the man who claimed to be the Son of God. The plot thickened while Jesus was in Bethany, at the house of Simon the leper. A woman entered the room and poured precious ointment from an alabaster box on the head of Jesus. Suddenly money became the focal point for some of the disciples. They became aware that the poor needed help and suggested that the ointment might better have been sold and the money given to the poor. In other words, they suggested it was a waste to pour ointment on the head of Jesus.

Judas Iscariot, one of the twelve disciples, grasped the idea and decided to make some money for himself. He secretly entered into an agreement with the chief priests, scribes, and elders, offering to sell Jesus. When he asked what would be given to him if he delivered Jesus up to them, they covenanted with him for thirty pieces of silver.

This was a basic verbal contract between Judas and the chief priests. There was a meeting of the minds, although Judas probably was unaware that he was becoming a party to a contract. The *Merriam-Webster Dictionary* gives the meaning of "covenant" as a formal, binding agreement— the same definition it gives for the word "contract." The agreement between Judas and the chief priest was binding. The offer was final. This contract did not contain a cancellation clause. The deal was done for what it was worth to Judas.

Jesus probably was not betrayed for gain or wealth. Otherwise, Judas would have demanded a greater price. He no doubt intended to scam the chief priest when he received the thirty pieces of silver. He probably thought that Jesus would raise His hand and His assailants would fall to the ground, giving Jesus a chance to escape.

But this was not the case. When Jesus returned from praying and found his disciples asleep, He said to Peter, "What, could ye not watch with me one hour? Watch and pray that ye enter not into temptation: the spirit indeed is willing, but the flesh is weak." Jesus was speaking about the weakness of the flesh and its inability to withstand the pressure of physical requirements. He was likewise alluding to the susceptibility of human nature to temptation.

At the Last Supper, Judas was the one in charge of the money bag. This afforded him the opportunity to conduct financial transactions. He no doubt purchased the wine and the bread for the meal and paid the rent for the upper room. Judas could have remained with the other disciples and enjoyed fellowship with Jesus, but he opted for an easy payday. He did not know that this was a scheme that would not be financially beneficial to him. He soon found out that his attempt to sell the truth had been a horrible mistake. The scam had serious repercussions for the scammer.

When Jesus was taken prisoner, Judas began to question his actions. "What have I done?" He realized that there was a greater conspiracy in the works, a conspiracy to buy the truth and destroy it before it became too powerful. He regretted his agreement and tried to return the thirty pieces of silver to the chief priest. Judas had not understood that the contract into which he entered was irrevocable. The chief priest and elders had very harsh words for him, saying, "What is that to us? See thou to that."

Judas, forced to acknowledge that he could not reverse his action, repented himself, threw the money down in the temple, and confessed his sin of having betrayed innocent blood. He then went out and hanged himself. Judas probably thought that by doing so, he could avoid shame and degradation for his sin.

> But all this was done that the scriptures of the prophets might be fulfilled. (Matt. 26:56)

> Buy the truth, and sell *it* not; *also* wisdom, and instruction, and understanding. (Prov. 23:23)

Why is money being made such a big factor in the evangelical system today? A semblance of an answer can be found in the gospel of Matthew. When Jesus was at variance with the ideals of the Pharisees, they tried to trap Him into either dishonoring the Roman emperor or blaspheming against God:

> Tell us therefore, what thinkest thou? Is it lawful to give tribute unto Caesar, or not?
>
> But Jesus perceived their wickedness and said. Why tempt me, ye hypocrites?
>
> Show me the tribute money. And they brought unto Him a penny.
>
> And He saith unto them, whose is this image and superscription?
>
> They say unto Him, Caesar's. Then saith he unto them, Render therefore unto Caesar the things which are Caesar's and unto God the things that are God's. (Matt. 22:17–21)

When Jesus sent out his twelve disciples to preach and to teach, He gave them power over unclean spirits and commanded that they take nothing for their journey, save a staff. They could carry no script, no bread, and no money in their purses. "Ye should be shod with sandals; and not put on two coats" (Mark 6:7–9).

Televangelist organizations are registered as nonprofit businesses, and they require money to function. But the way they play upon the words of the Bible to satisfy their financial greed is very misleading. For instance, some use the word "seed" (referenced in Leviticus 27:30) to imply that you are required to "sow a thousand-dollar seed" to obtain God's blessing. This is downright ludicrous.

One preacher claims that God does not respond to our needs, but to our faith. If this were the case, why would the Bible state that God will supply our needs according to His riches in glory?

The same preacher said that tithing does not guarantee prosperity—tithing with expectation guarantees prosperity. There is a vast difference between the method of tithing mentioned in the Old Testament and the method used in our time. However, the promise to give the tithe was made by Jacob in the book of Genesis based upon God's promised blessings to him and his seed. It was a promise made as an acknowledgment of God's blessings and not as an expectation of prosperity. When someone grants you a favor, you say thank you. When someone sends you a gift, you send that person a thank-you card. How much more, when God blesses you, should you not say thank you by making a sacrifice?

> And Jacob went out from the land of Beersheba and went toward Haran.
>
> And he lighted upon a certain place and tarried there all night because the sun was set; and he took of the stones of that place, and put them for his pillows, and lay down there to sleep.

And he dreamed, and behold a ladder set up on the earth, and the top of it reached to heaven: and behold the angels of God ascending and descending on it. (Gen. 28:10–12 KJV)

And behold, the Lord stood above it, and said, I am the Lord God of Abraham thy father, and the God of Isaac: the land whereon thou liest, to thee will I give it, and to thy seed.

And thy seed shall be as the dust of the earth, and thou shalt spread abroad to the west, and to the east, and to the north, and to the south: and in thee and in all thy seed shall all the families of the earth be blessed.

And, behold, I am with thee, and will keep in all places wither thou goest, and will bring again this land; for I will not leave thee, until I have done that which I have spoken to thee of. (Gen. 28:13–15 KJV)

And Jacob vowed a vow, saying, If God will be with me, and will keep me in this way that I go, and will give me bread to eat, and raiment to put on.

So that I come again to my father's house in peace; then shall the Lord be my God:

And this stone which I have set for a pillar shall be God's house: and of all that thou shalt give me I will surely give the tenth unto thee. (Gen. 28:20–22 KJV)

This was clearly a promise of condition made by Jacob after God communicated with him in a dream and informed him of the blessings that would be extended to him and his seed. The magnitude of the blessing was obvious from the vastness of Jacob's seed. It was as the dust of the earth, spreading to the east and to the west and to the north and to the south.

No demands were made by God, only a promise of blessings. Therefore, the vow made by Jacob to give a tenth of the blessings that he would receive from God was an act of gratitude. This was a personal decision made by Jacob. As head of household, it was his right to pass on to his seed the act of showing gratitude to God. The concept of tithing seems simple as set forth in Leviticus:

> And all the tithe of the land, whether of the seed of the land, or of the fruit of the tree, is the Lord's: It is holy unto the lord. (Lev. 27:30 KJV)

> And concerning the tithe of the herd, or of the flock, even of whatsoever passeth under the rod, the tenth shall be holy unto the Lord. (Lev. 27:32 KJV)

> These are the commandments, which the Lord commanded Moses for the children of Israel in Mount Sinai. (Lev. 27:34 KJV)

Instructions for the tithe were further explained in the book of Numbers: "And the Lord spake unto Moses saying, 'Thus speak unto the Levites and say unto them, When ye take of the children of Israel the tithes which I have given you from them for your inheritance, then ye shall offer up an heave offering of it for the Lord even a tenth part of the tithe'" (Num. 18:25–26 KJV).

This was not tithing with expectation. It was tithing after reception. In other words, after the Israelites received their inheritance, they were required to give an offering of it for the Lord. "Thou mayest not eat within thy gates the tithe of thy corn, or of thy wine, or of thy oil, or the firstlings of thy herd or of thy flock, nor any of thy vows which thou vowest, nor thy freewill offerings, or heave offering of thy hand" (Deut. 12:17 KJV).

No wonder the televangelists hardly ever preach from the books of Leviticus or Deuteronomy. They choose to stress the parts of the book of Malachi that speak about the act and benefits of tithing.

The suggestion that God will only bless us if we give a tenth of our finances to the church is misleading. In the dispensation before Christ, wages were not necessarily paid with money, and trade or barter was not always made with silver or gold. For example, Jacob lived at his uncle Laban's home for some time and performed service in return for his kindness. Laban wanted to pay Jacob and inquired what wages Jacob wanted. Jacob wanted to receive Laban's younger daughter Rachel as his payment. But Laban had another daughter who was older than Rachel. Her name was Leah. Since it was not the custom for the younger sister to be married before the older, Laban preferred to give Leah to Jacob for his service. This is what Laban did. Jacob, however, loved Rachel and offered to serve an additional seven years to receive her. Jacob worked for Laban faithfully for fourteen years and received two wives as his wages. Was Jacob required to give a tenth of his wages as a sacrifice to God?

The book of Malachi explains the basic principle of the tithe. The tithe (tenth) was a small part of the harvest that was required to be given as a sacrificial offering to God—not for His personal use, but for the benefit of others. "'Bring me all the tithes into the storehouse, that there may be meat in mine house and prove me now herewith,' saith the Lord of host, 'if I will not open you the windows of heaven, and pour you out a blessing, that there shall not be room enough to receive it'" (Mal. 3:10 KJV)

According to instructions given by God to Moses, the Israelites were required to give a tenth of their harvest as a sacrificial offering to the Lord in return for God's favor. The sacrificial offering was not limited to crops, but also included animals or anything that the Israelites wanted to dedicate to the Lord as a way of thanking Him for sending the rain ("I will open the windows of heaven and pour you out a blessing"), which was bestowed upon the land to bring about large increase in the crops. An offering of righteousness was the requirement from the sons of Levi. The gold and silver mentioned, along with the refiner's fire and fuller's soap, represent the quality and purity of their offering.

One televangelist, while speaking to a very large audience, has used that scriptural passage to influence his audience to donate a thousand dollars. He said, "If you would release the [thousand dollar] seed that is in your hand, God will release the seed that is in His hand."[1] He spoke about his personal experiences and the many blessings that he received. The blessings began when he gave his first thousand dollars to the church. The gifts included cars, suits, and even money from various persons. I am sure they were not old suits nor old cars. His implication was that only those who gave a thousand dollars or more would be blessed by God. Are we to believe that God's blessings are for sale?

---

[1] The Inspirational Camp Meeting (BET TV)

This same preacher said that tithing does not guarantee prosperity; tithing with expectation guarantees prosperity. Are we to believe that he expected those brand-new Corvettes, BMWs, Rolex watches, and suits when he gave his first thousand dollars to the church?

He also said that he has clothes in his closet with the price tags still on them. It is a shame that he can boast about something like that when there are so many people out there who are in need. I am sure that most, if not all, of those people to whom he was preaching had paid their tithes faithfully and were still driving their old cars. They had not gotten a new watch or new outfit and could not afford to buy any.

My understanding is that all tithes given to the church are to be used for spreading the gospel by way of radio, television, renovation of current churches, and construction of new churches for the benefit of those people who do not know Jesus as their Lord and Savior. Tithes are not intended as an investment in hope of a personal profit. "Buy the truth, and sell *it* not; *also* wisdom, and instruction, and understanding" (Prov. 23:23 KJV).

CHAPTER 3

THE SIGNATURE: THE WRITING ON THE WALL

In the book of Daniel, King Belshazzar thought he could buy the truth. King Belshazzar, his princes, his wives, and his concubines defiled the gold and silver vessels that his father, Nebuchadnezzar, had removed from the temple in Jerusalem, by drinking wine from them. While they drank, they praised their gods of gold, silver, brass, iron, wood, and stone (Dan. 5:4).

However, Belshazzar was in for a rude awakening. At that same hour, there appeared the fingers of a man's hand, which wrote upon the plaster of the wall of the king's palace. This strange phenomenon worried the king to the point that his countenance fell and his knees knocked against each other. In frustration, he called for the astrologers, the Chaldeans, and the soothsayers and said, "Whosoever shall read this writing and shew me the interpretation thereof, shall be clothe in scarlet, and have a chain of gold about his neck, and shall be the third ruler in the kingdom."

Despite their wisdom, the king's wise men could not read the writing or make known to the king the interpretation thereof. The queen sought to come to his rescue. She told him about a man who possessed very high qualifications:

> There is a man in thy kingdom, in whom is the spirit of the holy gods; and in the days of thy father light and understanding and wisdom. Like the wisdom of the gods, was found in him; whom the king Nebuchadnezzar thy father, the king; I say, thy father, made master of the magicians, astrologers, Chaldeans, and soothsayers;

> Forasmuch as an excellent spirit, and knowledge, and understanding, interpreting of dreams, and shewing of hard sentences, and dissolving of doubts, were found in the same Daniel, whom the king named Belteshazzar: now let Daniel be called, and he will shew the interpretation.

> Then was Daniel brought in before the king, and the king spake and said unto Daniel, Art thou that Daniel, which art of the children of the captivity of Judah, whom the king my father brought out of Jewry?

> I have even heard of thee, that the spirit of the gods is in thee, and that light and understanding and excellent wisdom is found in thee.

And now the wise men, the astrologers, have brought in before me, that they should read this writing, and make known unto me the interpretation thereof: but they could not shew the interpretation of the thing:

And I have heard of thee that thou canst make interpretations, and dissolve doubts: now if thou canst read the writing, and make known unto me the interpretation thereof, thou shalt be clothed with scarlet, and have a chain of gold about thy neck, and shalt be the third ruler in the kingdom.

Then Daniel answered and said before the king. Let thy gifts be to thyself, and give thy rewards to another; yet I will read the writing unto the king and make known to him the interpretation. (Dan. 5:11–17)

In this scenario, King Belshazzar found himself in the same position as his father. He became the mirror reflection of his father, King Nebuchadnezzar. Having been blessed with wealth and power, he lacked one thing—humility. His father had not heeded the warning he received in a dream, and suffered the consequences of his arrogance. Belshazzar also received a warning, but his wealth got in the way of his reason. He thought the truth could be bought. "Buy the truth, and sell *it* not; *also* wisdom, and instruction, and understanding" (Prov. 23:23 KJV).

Some televangelists are selective when preaching about tithing. They often place emphasis on the part in the book of Malachi that asks, "Will a man rob God? Yet ye have robbed me. But ye say, wherein have we robbed thee? In tithes and offerings" (Mal. 3:8 KJV). There is quite a bit of rhetoric in this chapter, since the questions are asked and then the responses follow.

Some time ago, a televangelist was preaching to his congregation, and he chided the female members about their lack of tithing. He said, "You are walking in here wearing your fancy hats and stylish dresses while not paying your tithes. That is God's money you are spending."

Meanwhile, in another service, this same preacher stated that he had never flown on a commercial airline and that he used a private jet to travel all over the world. As a matter of fact, he recently asked his congregation for sixty-five thousand dollars for a new jet, so he could continue doing God's work around the world.

While I am not questioning his wealth, I draw the distinction between his money and, as he termed the tithe, "God's money." "Wilt thou set thine eyes upon that which is not? For riches certainly make themselves wings; they fly away as an eagle towards heaven" (Prov. 23:5 KJV).

Is it a coincidence that this televangelist displayed his massive home and expensive suits and claimed that he must have a jet to do the Lord's work; therefore, the congregation must make sure to give the money for that jet? Does he ever read Proverbs 23:5?

There was once a gentleman who had worn out the soles of his shoes and could not afford to purchase another pair. But he did not miss church on Sunday; he simply got dressed in his suit and walked barefooted to church. Yes! You guessed it! He still paid his tithes. This is the type of ridiculous contrast that exists in some churches.

Tithing is not meant to be a burden on anyone. Tithes should only be given and treated as a return in appreciation for all the blessings God has bestowed upon us. Tithes should be used to help others to understand that God has invested in us, and we should show our gratitude for the sacrifice He made. Tithing should never be used as a deposit with the expectation of a windfall return on our investment.

This reminds us of the conversation Jesus had with the Pharisees in the book of Matthew when they inquired about the superscription on a coin. Jesus said, "Render therefore unto Caesar the things which are Caesar's and unto God the things that are God's" (Matt. 22:21 KJV). This clearly tells us that God does not require money. All He needs is for us to worship, love, and honor Him. Jesus also said that it is easier for a camel to pass through the eye of a needle than for a rich man to enter heaven.

There are various methods and topics used by televangelists to capture the imaginations of their audiences. Some speak about healing, some speak about wealth, and some speak about salvation and faith in God. Those who preach about healing offer what they call "holy spring water" that is sent with special instructions that you must follow. They claim that the water comes from a place in the Holy Land.

Used correctly, the water is supposed to provide healing for whatever ails you.

These healing preachers provide witnesses who testify to their experience of being healed. Some claim they no longer need to use walking canes. Some have discarded their wheelchairs. Some claim to be healed from cancer. Others claim to have been set free from drug use.

Some preachers offer a prayer cloth that must be used according to instructions provided and then returned to the sender. Some offer to pray for anyone who calls their prayer center phone number.

While my intent is not to cast aspersions on these televangelists and their methods of operation, I still must wonder about their financial prowess. Those who preach about financial success usually incorporate the need for us to accept Christ into our lives through faith in God. This will in turn enable us to receive God's financial blessing.

Tithing was part of God's laws given to the children of Israel by Moses, and had nothing to do with money. Many later churches celebrated the harvest, when people would make contributions from whatever crops they had. The day following the harvest, their contributions would be redistributed to the poorest in the community. Some churches sold whatever donated produce remained after redistribution and used the proceeds to assist in the administration of the church. Most of these churches eventually discontinued the harvest festival. Some of them implemented a new system by placing a box for donations.

There is now an organization in New York City called City Harvest that collects donations of food and redistributes it to the hungry.

After the children of Israel suffered so much at the hands of Pharaoh, they became rebellious and disorderly on their way to the Promised Land. Moses, being the only ruler at that time, had the responsibility of enforcing the laws of God, judging the people, and providing solutions to their problems. Since there were many commandments, laws, and ordinances given by God, Moses would sit to judge the people for an entire day. That could be tiresome.

Jethro, Moses's father-in-law, happened to be visiting him, and observed the way Moses conducted his daily administration. Jethro provided counsel on the matter. "And Moses' father in law said unto him. The thing that thou doest is not good. … Harken now unto my voice. I will give counsel, and God will be with thee: Be thou for the people to God-ward, that thou mayest bring the curses unto God: And thou shall teach them ordinances and laws, and shalt shew them the way wherein they must walk, and the work that they must do" (Exod. 18:17, 19–20 KJV).

There has never been, in the sense that Moses did it, an in-depth teaching by televangelists about tithing. They only complain about members not paying their tithes, which are required for the Lord's work to progress. Some televangelists are very good, inspirational speakers and provide us with great stories and tips for daily living. A few of them even fill us in on their life experiences, showing how their circumstances changed from poverty to a life of fulfillment.

There was a televangelist I admired and loved to hear speak. My wife and I would watch his service every Sunday morning. He had a beautifully designed church building that I am sure cost a handsome amount to build. He often offered books for sale, and sometimes he gave books to people who made special money gifts to the church. He created membership groups, to which he gave names such as the Sparrows and the Eagles. Membership in these clubs could be obtained for an annual donation of a specified amount. The church gave a special gift to new members. Famous people often were invited as guest speakers, which brought prestige to the church.

Some televangelists have even gone to Hollywood, doing reality television shows and acting in movies. I have seen this scenario acted out on national television in a program called *Preachers of LA* on the Oxygen cable network. In one episode, a preacher claimed that he had been a drug user and was seen returning to the hood and speaking with his former friends, trying to encourage them to accept salvation. He was dressed flamboyantly, drove an expensive car, lived in a luxurious home, and had a separate house as his man cave. He drove a different car for trips to his man cave, where he met his fellow preachers to have discussions or simply hang out. These men likewise led magnificent churches with large memberships.

Can you imagine the money they are making from such a business?

On one occasion, one pastor criticized another about his style of travel—the accused man had an entourage, including bodyguards. The contention was that Jesus never had an entourage, only followers. He never carried a gun and needed no protection.

The same argument, however, can be made about expensive cars and aircraft. Jesus never had those either. He, his disciples, and later missionaries traveled on foot and by boat, yet they never complained. Neither did they ask for financial assistance from their followers.

We would do well to remember the apostle Paul as a perfect example. He never requested financial help from the churches in the cities where he taught and preached. He accepted only whatever gifts were offered to him. There is no record of him offering any of his teachings for sale. The important aspects of his life were spiritual rather than financial. Paul believed in the sufficiency of Christ, and made that point clear when he wrote to the church at Philippi: "But I rejoice in the Lord greatly, that now at the last your care of me hath flourished again; wherein ye were also careful, but ye lacked opportunity. Not that I speak in respect of want: for I have learned, in whatever state I am, therewith to be content" (Phil. 4:10–11 KJV).

Paul expressed a quality that I find lacking in many evangelists today. To be content whatever his physical state is an attitude that speaks volumes and should be an example for us to follow. Paul was aware that his followers were willing to provide him with assistance but, because of their own inadequacies, did not always find that possible. Yet Paul continued his mission without complaining.

Today, the more we give, the more the televangelists want. They introduce a new book each month as their gift to us for our monthly support. I once visited a church where they introduced the offertory three times during the same service. There are always special reasons given for the collection of more money: building repairs, a larger lot, a new piano or organ, or even the celebration of the pastor's birthday.

Televangelists use their preaching and motivational speaking to encourage audiences to pay for their extravagant lifestyles. Show me a televangelist who lives in a rented apartment or owns a modest family home and one car, and I will show you a person dedicated to the work of God and the spiritual needs of the people.

These TV preachers tell us that we must be positive and expect great things. We must continue to believe that better times are coming. Every year they say to us, "This is your year!" Everything we are hoping for will be accomplished according to our faith, they say, as stated in the book of Hebrews: "Now faith is the substance of things hope for, the evidence of things not seen."

I am sure that their philosophy is that once we believe all things are possible, our lives will be changed for the better—and as a result, we will make bigger contributions. I believe that some of these televangelists can do a lot more than they are doing to help alleviate hunger and homelessness in the world.

Moses's responsibility was to teach the people the ordinances and laws of God: "And thou shall teach them ordinances and laws, and shalt shew them the way wherein they must walk, and the work that they must do" (Exod. 18:20 KJV). It seems, however, that televangelists consider it their primary responsibility to collect money from the people.

CHAPTER 4

HISTORIC ROOTS
OF SACRIFICE

The Old Testament contains an extensive and technical vocabulary dealing with sacrifices and offerings. The prescribed rituals were a major means of expressing worshippers' faith. Rituals were one of God's means for illustrating the nature of the Israelites' relationship with him. Old Testament ritual involved offerings, in that everything brought for use in worship was viewed as having been offered to God, and thus was set apart and holy (Exod. 28:38). The ritual system also featured sacrifice. The most significant offerings called for the sacrifice of a living animal. Throughout the Bible, sacrifice was the avenue by which a sinning humanity approached a holy God.

The practice of sacrifice precedes establishment of Mosaic Law. Many believe that the first sacrifice was God's killing of an animal to provide skin covering for Adam and Eve after the fall (Gen. 3:21). The story of Cain and Abel indicates that the way to approach God with sacrifice may have been made clear to the first family (Gen. 4). Cain "brought some of the fruits of the soil as an offering to the Lord. But Abel brought fat portions from some of the firstborn of his flock.

The Lord looked with favor on Abel and his offering, but on Cain and his offering he did not look with favor."

God's rebuke to an angry Cain was "If you do what is right would you not be accepted?" This suggests that Cain's sacrifice was made in conscious violation of God's known will.

Cain and Abel, by offering up to God a portion of the benefits of their labor, tried to repair the broken relationship between their parents and God. Adam and Eve had disobeyed God and were driven out of the garden of Eden. While their motive was genuine, it became flawed because it ended with AHEM—anger, hatred, envy, and murder. Although the offering of the first fruits of the land is an accepted form of sacrifice to God, it is not the quintessential sacrifice. In the same manner, though the offerings of money that we give to the church sacrificially are accepted, these are not the same as the sacrifice of God's Son on the cross of Calvary, where He died to atone for our sins.

David seems to express the ineffectiveness of animal sacrifice in Psalm 51:

> For thou desirest not sacrifice; else would I give it: thou delightest not in burnt offering.
>
> The sacrifices of God are a broken spirit: a broken and contrite heart, O God, thou wilt not despise. (Ps. 51:16–17)

Some ministers use money as a topic in almost every sermon. I do not decry the churches for their efforts to obtain monetary gifts to advance their ministries. St. Paul accepted gifts to aid him in his ministerial journeys. But he never made any demands or requested any specific amounts.

What I am against are the methods televangelists use and the way the money is being utilized. If ministers' salaries are paid from the tithes and offerings, why do their salaries afford them the means to wear seven-hundred-dollar suits, live in million-dollar homes, and drive luxurious cars? Some of the church members who pay those tithes live in rental homes, wear inexpensive clothes, and drive secondhand cars.

Another observation is the questionable presence of ATMs in the lobbies of some church buildings. These machines do not dispense Bibles or hymnbooks. The only thing that can be obtained from them is money, and they do not provide small change either. Maybe they are there for the wayward person without a wallet or purse who happens to be passing by the church and is drawn in by the Holy Spirit. If that person wishes to make a purchase or donate, then the ATM will serve that purpose.

I am sure that the average member who attends a service does so with the understanding that they are expected to participate in the offertory, and arrives prepared to do so. Therefore, an ATM in the lobby is irrelevant. It relegates the church to a place of business rather than a place of worship.

But can we really separate the business part of these organizations from the religious part? Every one of these organizations has a governing body: a board of directors, a president, a secretary, a treasurer, an accountant, and whatever other staff they may have. Do all these people volunteer their time?

No. These organizations are not-for-profit. Therefore, any remuneration this staff receives cannot be called salary, only a stipend. They all receive stipends. Where does the money for stipends come from?

For a business to survive, it must be liquid and able to maintain liquidity. After overhead is recouped and all expenditures met, the remaining money becomes a profit— or maybe we should say that it becomes a gain, since the word "profit' sounds like a wheel-and-deal situation.

In the financial sector, stockbrokers were formerly called "dealers" because of the method they employed to make their business profitable. They would buy stock at a low price and then sell it at a higher price. That is where the term "wheel and deal" came in. Hence stockbrokers were called dealers. Because of the negative connotation, that name was changed to "brokers."

Before we label televangelical organizations as profiteering enterprises, we must first define the word "profit." The *Merriam-Webster Dictionary* defines "profit" as a valuable return or gain, or the excess of the selling price of goods over their cost.

So again I ask, what are the televangelists selling? Inspirational books for daily living and sermons reproduced on CDs? If what they are selling represents the truth, who can determine its cost or value? Can the truth really be bought or sold? "Buy the truth, and sell *it* not; *als*o wisdom, and instruction, and understanding" (Prov. 23:23 KJV).

Most televangelical organizations are not only businesses, they are family businesses. When some of them were formed, the edict was that if the founder should die or retire, then the order of succession must pass to that founder's legal heir, even if that person is not fully equipped for the job. The object is to secure the longevity of the family business. If that were not so, why would they incorporate the family name into the organization name? Why not use another name like Many Days Evangelical Association or FreetoGrowMoney.org?

The late Dr. Harold Camden stated in one of his broadcasts that the church no longer exists, that it has been dissolved.[2] Whether one believes this to be true or not, I do agree that the church no longer exists the way we used to know it. Gone are the hymnbooks and congregational singing; in are jumbo screens and trained choruses. Gone are the hellfire and brimstone preaching and the call for sinners to repent. In are inspirational speaking and affiliation suggestions to join a spiritually grounded church. Gone are the missionaries who traveled independently to other countries to spread the gospel. In are cruises and service on cruise liners.

We know that those cruises are not for free. They must be paid for. But of course we know the deal: the minister and

---

[2] Family Radio

his family get theirs for free. There is nothing objectionable about this scenario. It is quite okay for an organization to raise funds to further its ministry. However, when it comes to selling sermons, I must draw the line. Sermons may be personal thoughts, but once their basis in Scripture is claimed, then they are being portrayed as truth. The Bible tells us that we must not buy or sell the truth, also wisdom and understanding.

"How be it when he, the spirit of truth, is come, he shall guide you into all truth for he shall not speak of himself; but whatsoever he shall hear, that shall he speak, and he shall show you things to come" (John 16:13 KJV). Here we see the personification of the spirit of truth by Jesus. If the spirit of truth is identified as a person, then how can truth be offered for sale and bought? Can we place the spirit of truth in the same category as we would a book or CD?

There are many reasons that sound acceptable for raising money, especially if stated by someone professing a strong spiritual dedication. The reason most often used is the need to help the poor. A perfect example of this is found in the gospel of Matthew:

> Now when Jesus was in Bethany, in the house of Simon the leper. There came unto him a woman having a box of very precious ointment, and poured it on his head, as he sat at meat. But when his disciples saw it, they had indignation, saying. To what purpose is this waste? For this ointment might have been sold for much and given

> to the poor. When Jesus understood it, he said unto them, why trouble ye the woman? For she hath wrought a good work upon me. For ye have the poor with you always but me ye have not always. (Matt. 26:6–11 KJV)

We can well imagine the wealth of this woman who thought it a great privilege to be able to pour a box of precious ointment on the head of Jesus. It is noteworthy that the ones who supposedly were the closest to Jesus were the ones who had the most negative reaction.

Why would the disciples be so indignant about the woman's actions? Was it about the use of the ointment? Was it about its value? Although nothing was said about its cost, I believe it was a very expensive ointment, because it was described as precious.

Here we see a perfect example of an attempt to exploit the poor. It took a woman with a box of expensive ointment to arouse the disciples' interest in the poor. Jesus saw through their indignant words and said, "Ye have the poor with you always." In other words, why did you wait until now to realize that there are poor people who need help? They were always there.

This woman could well have said to the disciples, "It's not for sale." However, she was focused on her commitment. She knew that her spiritual relationship with Jesus was more important than the value of the ointment or the money that could be obtained from its sale, even though the suggested use was to help the poor. The point is not that the poor are unimportant. The point is that she had a unique opportunity to satisfy her spiritual hunger, and that is more important.

The intent of this book is not to castigate the televangelists, but to show that there can be misgivings about their methods of operation and the vast amount of money they acquire from their audience. What reasons are they giving for wanting to raise so much money? Are they exploiting the poor? Are they using the homeless and unemployed? They often use topics which will captivate people.

For instance, one preacher on national television preached about poverty and wealth and offered his book *God's Ancient Secret: The Shocking Truth about Prosperity Thinking* to anyone who called his advertised phone number.[3] He also offered his special oil and had people testify that they had received financial blessings after using the oil.

There was also another televangelist who claimed that God told him to send what he called "holy oil" to the first 288 people who called his advertised number while the program was being aired.[4] This exhortation leaves one to wonder why there is a stipulation. Does it have to do with the limited vials of holy oil? Or is it a limitation on the number of people God wants to help?

The preacher's claims also created the impression that this so-called "holy oil" was a medium between the people and

---

[3] BET

[4] Ibid

God. The Bible states, "There is only one mediator between man and God, the man Christ Jesus."

Many people claimed to have received large financial blessings, as the preacher had said they would, after using the oil. One person testified that she had won a large sum of money. Another person claimed that her mortgage was miraculously paid off. Someone also claimed to be free from drug addiction after using the oil. Not once did anyone claim that their faith in God was the reason for their blessings. While I am not questioning the witnesses' faith, I wonder why they were required to use "holy oil" to achieve those results.

During Jesus's ministry on earth, He performed many miracles. He raised the dead, healed the sick, caused the lame to walk, and made the blind to see. But never did He impose any requirement other than the exercise of their faith.

The woman with the issue of blood was a perfect example of faith in action. Her desire was to be healed, and she believed that touching Jesus's garment would provide that healing. We must bear in mind that touching the garment did not provide the healing; it was her faith that healed her. If she had not believed, then even though she touched the garment, she would not have experienced the healing. Jesus said to her, "Thy faith has made thee whole." Jesus did not make any demands on her. There were no requirements to meet. There was never a question of whether she tithed or even visited a temple. She had what was important for her healing—her faith. This was expectation without tithing and not tithing with expectation.

Compare this to the words of the Inspirational Camp Meeting preacher Mike Murdock, who told the story of a man who claimed that he did not tithe with the expectation of receiving anything.[5] Dr. Murdock replied by singing, "How dumb thou art, how dumb thou art" (to the tune of "How Great Thou Art").

While he does not stress the act of tithing, Dr. Murdock believes in sowing thousand-dollar seeds to reap a harvest. He also believes in praying a Boaz blessing for callers: that whatever blessings he receives, they will also receive. However, that prayer is incumbent upon sowing the thousand-dollar seed. If the thousand-dollar seed sown really generates a harvest, then why would he have to pray for them to receive a Boaz blessing—or any blessing, for that matter?

I have spent quite a bit of time discussing the topic of tithing, which, however, is beside the point. What is more important is my concern with the methods used by megachurches to obtain money from their audiences. An even greater concern is the way the money is being spent. When these preachers ply their wares from their pulpits, there can only be a single intent, and that is to maximize their profits.

Oops! I forgot that we cannot say "profits" because they are not-for-profit organizations.

---

[5] BET

Meanwhile there are poor people praying in the congregation who are unable to pay their rent or even prepare themselves a proper meal. They probably do not have a thousand dollars in their bank accounts. Maybe they do not even have bank accounts.

The megachurches did not spring up overnight. Every megachurch was once a grassroots church with a small congregation. It took time, energy, and money to implement the transformation from minor to major. Time, we know they had; energy, we assume they had; but money? The question is, where did the money come from? How can a small congregation make a down payment on an old football stadium or a plot of land to construct a massive building? Banks are in business of lending money, but to acquire a loan, one must still provide collateral.

We can make all the assumptions we care to make, but there is one sure way to amass money that sticks out in my mind—sales. Megachurches sell books, DVDs, and event tickets. But the best moneymaker is the sale of the truth from the pulpit and on media. Are those preachers oblivious to what the Bible says? "Buy the truth, and sell *it* not; *also* wisdom, and instruction, and understanding" (Prov. 23:23).

It appears that they will use any means possible to raise money for their luxurious lifestyle, to the point where their actions make it possible for anyone to denigrate the meaning of the church.

Consider Indiana's First Church of Cannabis, a sect that embraces marijuana use as a sacrament, newly formed under the state's controversial Religious Freedom Restoration Act. It has just received the classification that many religious organizations covet: tax-exempt status under section 501(c)(3) of the Internal Revenue Service code.[6]

I can well imagine the number of people rushing to become members of Indiana's First Church of Cannabis. Marijuana has taken on a new identity. Among pharmaceutical companies and medical practitioners, it is now prescribed as medical marijuana. This church has adopted it as a sacrament, so it can now be called sacramental marijuana. Is this a real church? And if it is, how many others will follow this system to maximize their membership, since more members mean more money?

Separation of Church and State: The Metaphor and the Constitution

"Separation of church and state" is a common metaphor that is well recognized. Equally well recognized is the metaphor's meaning: the church will stay out of the state's business and the state will stay out of the church's business.

Because of the very common usage of the phrase, most people incorrectly think it is written in the Constitution. The phrase "wall of separation between the church and the state" was originally coined by Thomas Jefferson in a letter to the Danbury Baptists on January 1, 1802. His purpose in

[6]   http://www.huffingtonpost.com/2015/06/02/indianas-church-of-marijuana_n_7496084.html?icid=maing-grid7%7Cmain5%7Cdl3%7Csec3_lnk4%26pLid%3D-1253548193

this letter was to assuage the fears of the congregation, and so he told them that this wall had been erected to protect them. He used the metaphor exclusively to mean keeping the state out of the church's business, not keeping the church out of the state's business.

The Constitution states, "Congress shall make no law respecting an establishment of religion or prohibiting the free exercise thereof." Both the free-exercise clause and the establishment clause place restrictions on the government concerning laws that might interfere with religion. No restrictions are placed on religions, except perhaps that a religious denomination cannot become the state religion.

However, currently the common understanding of the metaphor is strictly for the church to stay out of the state's business. The original meaning essentially cannot be found in the media, the judiciary, or in public debate, and is not part of the agenda of the ACLU.

The problem is that the Constitution failed to make a clear statement with regard to the financial viability of the church. While the government may not decide which religious organization has a right to claim not-for-profit status, the government should still be able to investigate the claim with regard to tax exemption. Most of these churches make a lot of money from the sale of media and from financial gifts. This money is not always used for the expenses of the church. So why should such organizations be given a free ride upon the backs of purchasers and donors? It is true that individuals can claim a deduction on donations made to a religious organization, but there is a limit to the amount they can claim. Meanwhile the organization can claim tax exemption under section 501(c)(3) regardless of the amount of money they receive.

Today's church is not the one Jesus spoke of when He spoke to Peter.

> When Jesus came into the coast of Caesarea Philippi, he asked his disciples, saying, whom do men say that I the son of man am?
>
> And they said, some say that thou art John the Baptist: some, Elias; and others, Jeremias, or one of the prophets.
>
> He saith unto them, but who say ye that I am?
>
> And Simon Peter answered and said, Thou art the Christ, the Son of the living God.
>
> And Jesus Answered and said unto him, blessed art thou, Simon Barjona: for flesh and blood hath not revealed it unto thee, but my father which is in heaven.
>
> And I say also unto thee, that thou art Peter, and upon this rock I will build my church; and the gates of hell will not prevail against it. (Matt. 16:13–18 KJV)

Jesus was speaking of building a church that would withstand the onslaught of the enemy (Satan) when He said the gates of hell would not prevail against it. According to the *Merriam-Webster Dictionary*, the word "prevail" means to triumph. Therefore, Jesus was saying that He would build His church (the people of God) so strong that sin would not succeed against it. Peter's faith was the blueprint by which Jesus would build His church.

Remember that when the disciples were unsure about what others were saying concerning the identity of Jesus, Peter spoke up and said confidently, "Thou art the Christ, the Son of the living God." Peter had a personal revelation of who Jesus was and did not hesitate to share his experience.

The word "church" was never intended to mean the brick-and-mortar structures we worship in today. The church originated with Jesus. Places of worship were known as temples and synagogues, and there were other activities being conducted in those places too. Remember when Jesus whipped the moneychangers and ran them out of the temple? There was a basic reason for Jesus's stern rebuke of those people.

The reason was not that the moneychangers were doing business, because even though they were not doing physical labor, they were working. Work was a sentence imposed on Adam and Eve by God when they were expelled from the garden of Eden. They were told, "By the sweat of your brow shall ye eat bread."

The problem was not what the moneychangers did, but where they did it. "And Jesus went into the temple of God and cast out all them that sold and bought in the temple, and overthrew the tables of the money-changers, and the seats of them that sold doves. And said unto them, it is written. My house shall be called a house of prayer, but ye have made it a den of thieves" (Matt. 21:12–13 KJV).

CHAPTER 5

Money Matters

Does money really matter? Humanity has diverged from the original form of worship and lost all respect for the house of God, while becoming more obsessed with earthly wealth. We well remember the story of the rich man and Lazarus. There's also the story of the rich young ruler who came to Jesus and asked, "Good master, what must I do to inherit eternal life."

Jesus instructed the young ruler about obeying the commandments. The youth claimed that he obeyed them from childhood. Jesus responded, "Go sell all that you have and give to the poor." The young ruler went away sorrowful, for he had great wealth.

The importance of personal wealth is reflected in this young man's attitude toward the poor. He preferred to hold on to his riches, ignore the poor, and lose the opportunity to inherit eternal life. This young ruler could not accept the idea of relinquishing present success and prestige for the promise of future success and happiness. He had no faith in the unknown value of eternal life.

His decision and attitude caused Jesus to stress to His disciples the importance of righteousness and the danger of riches: "Then said Jesus unto his disciples. Verily I say unto you. That a rich man shall hardly enter the kingdom of heaven. And again I say unto you. It is easier for a camel to go through the eye of a needle, than for a rich man to enter the kingdom of God. When his disciples heard it, they were exceedingly amazed, saying, who then can be saved" (Matt. 19:23–25 KJV).

The disciples' reaction to Jesus's statement provides food for thought. What about the poor? Are they not eligible for entry into the kingdom of God? It seems that the disciples believed that only the rich could have access to the kingdom of God. In other words, they thought that eternal life was a commodity to be bought. These were the same disciples who suggested that the ointment poured out over Jesus's head could have been sold and the money given to the poor.

Jesus often spoke in parables. At one point while teaching the multitudes, He spoke about the deceitfulness of riches. Wealth was the downfall of many figures in the Bible; the business of economics was well established before Jesus came into the world. The word "profit" is used several times in the Bible, and on one occasion we are exposed to the stark reality of the possible negative consequences of doing business: "Then Jesus said unto his disciples, if any man will come after me, let him deny himself, and take up his cross, and follow me. For whosoever will save his life shall lose it: and whosoever shall lose his life for my sake shall find it. For what is a man profited, if he shall gain the whole world, and lose his own soul? Or what shall a man give in exchange for his soul?" (Matt. 16:24–26).

Note the words "profit," "gain," "lose," and "exchange." These words represent the fundamental basis of doing business. When televangelists offer CDs, books, and tickets for sale, they are directly or indirectly involved in doing business. Yet they claim to be nonprofit and obtain tax-exempt status under section 501(c)(3) of the Internal Revenue Code. There seems to be a vast difference between what the Constitution states and what the statement in the Constitution means.

You may wonder why I am discussing the Constitution and the church when the real focus in on the methods of televangelists: how they are obtaining the money they so lavishly display in their lifestyles. It is easy to misinterpret the Constitution, especially in terms of religion. There are two important words that must be taken into consideration. One is the word "restricting" and the other is the word "prohibiting."

According to the *Merriam-Webster Dictionary*, "restrict" is a verb that means to confine within boundaries. "Restriction" is a noun meaning something (such as a law or rule) that prevents an action or speech. These words have nothing to do with money; they have everything to do with the setting up of a place of residence or business. Since religious organizations are not recognized as businesses, then they can and should be categorized as residences. The implication here is that Congress cannot make any law that would prevent a church from organizing or expanding their establishment.

It is amazing how none of the televangelists ever preach about the danger of setting our eyes upon that (i.e., money) which is not. It is not evil for anyone to be rich, but riches may make us evil. Throughout the Bible, we are cautioned about the effects of riches, for good and bad. "Wilt thou set thine eyes upon that which is not? For riches certainly make themselves wings; they fly away as an eagle toward heaven" (Prov. 23:5 KJV). We have witnessed the truth in this Scripture verse when we see people who own private jets. One must be very rich to own a jet, and where do these jets go? They fly as eagles toward heaven. This is literal confirmation of that Scripture verse.

"The rich man is wise in his own conceit; but the poor that hath understanding searcheth him out" (Prov. 28:11). If we think about people we know who are rich, we will probably observe that some of them seem to be very conceited. They boast about their wealth, mainly because they know that they can buy whatever they want, own whatever they want or pay their way out of any unfortunate situation.

> Thus saith the Lord, let not the wise man glory in his wisdom, neither let the mighty man glory in his might, let not the rich man glory in his riches:
>
> But let him that glorieth glory in this, that he understandeth and knoweth me, that I am the Lord which exercise loving kindness, judgment, and righteousness, in the earth: for in these things I delight, sayeth the Lord. (Jer. 9:23–24)

> For we brought nothing into this world,
> and it is certain we can carry nothing out.
>
> And having food and raiment let us be
> therewith content.
>
> But they that will be rich, fall into
> temptation and a snare, and into many
> foolish and hurtful lusts, which drown
> men in destruction and perdition. (1 Tim.
> 6:7–9)
>
> For thus saith the Lord, ye have sold
> yourselves for nought; and ye shall be
> redeemed without money. (Isa. 52:3)

These are passages that seem to slip the minds of not only the televangelists, but also those pastors whose churches have very large congregations. Some of them become illicitly involved with female members of the church and lavish them with money and expensive gifts while the friendship lasts. When the friendship ends, they end up in court, with the pastor suing for repayment.

> There was a certain rich man, which was
> clothed in purple and fine linen, and feared
> sumptuously every day.
>
> And there was a certain beggar named
> Lazarus, which was laid at his gate, full of
> sores.

And desirous to be fed with the crumbs, which fell from the rich man's table: moreover, the dogs came and licked his sores.

And it came to pass, that the beggar died, and was carried by the angels into Abraham's bosom: the rich man also died and was buried. (Luke 16:19–22)

There you have it: money cannot replace the redemptive power of the blood of Christ. So when the televangelist tells you that you must tithe or commit to making a monetary donation of any amount to receive God's blessing, just think of Isaiah 52:3 and Luke 16:22.

Tithing was never instituted by God to be performed the way churches require it to be done. The tithe was to be used by the people themselves, since it was a tenth of whatever their fields produced. The difference between tithed produce and regular produce was that tithes were used in a special place chosen by God. If tithed goods were too heavy to carry to the designated place, they were sold for money, and the money used in the designated place (see Deut. 14:22).

Churches have adopted tithing because it is the surest way to get members to contribute a specific amount of their money to the church. While the amounts given differ according to the financial situation of the giver, it is at least 10 percent of whatever each one earns. If the situation were left to the members, probably some would give very little and some would give nothing.

The tithe, as referenced in Deuteronomy 14:22, was never meant for the use of the priest. It was to be used in a way that would express the people's appreciation of God's favor and all the blessings they received at His hand. They were to eat the tithe in a place designated by God. Eating of the tithe was a means of extending gratitude and providing privilege to those who were in need and were willing to accept the offer of God's mercy and grace.

CHAPTER 6

THE END TIME

Every day, because of the unrest and violence in the world, we are forced to wonder if we are approaching the end time. We have been warned that in the last days, perilous times will come, and that men will be lovers of themselves rather than lovers of God. Children will have children. Children will rise up against parents and parents against children. There will be wars and rumors of wars, earthquakes in diverse places, and wonders in heaven and on earth. There will be false prophets and those who will claim to be Christ. But we were given a consolation by Jesus when He said the end is not yet.

Every day we hear reports of a crisis in some part of the world, whether it be atmospheric, economic, humanitarian, political, military, or terror-related. Many countries are trying to stay above the fray by devaluing their currency. Many businesses are downsizing, and unemployment is skyrocketing. Anger is rampant, and guns are being used to solve many disputes. Almost every day there is news of a terrorist attack, the shooting down of a plane, or the detonation of a car bomb somewhere, resulting in the loss of many lives. Never have we seen so many court cases in which a parent is suing a child or a child suing a parent. We are forced to ask, are we in the tribulation period? Are we in the end time?

Recently, on October 29, 2012, there was a flood in New York City that devastated many lives. Homes were destroyed and people were afraid. It was said that there had not been a flood of this magnitude in the state of New York in a hundred years—but, as the saying goes, what has not happened in a hundred years can happen in a day, and it did. Maybe something of that magnitude will not happen for another hundred years, but how can we be sure?

For those of us who believe the Bible, we are provided with a parable about ten virgins attending a wedding. As the story goes, five were wise and five were foolish. The wise ones filled their lamps with oil and made sure they had an extra supply in preparation for the arrival of the bridegroom. The five foolish had only the oil in their lamps. As they waited for the bridegroom, they all fell asleep, and their lamps burned low. At midnight the bridegroom arrived, and the wise virgins were ready while the foolish were unprepared.

In New York City, families were devastated because of zoning errors. They thought they lived in a safe zone and did not seek higher ground, only to find themselves stranded without electricity, water, or food. The city was in a mess, and everyone seemed helpless. Again, we had a consolation: Jesus said that these things would happen, but the time is not yet.

If we read Genesis chapter six and compare our present time to the time before the Flood, the words of God are clear: "I will destroy man whom I have created from the face of the earth." If this does not cause us to think seriously about our lives and the way we live, then nothing will. In the days of Noah, the message was clear. Yet they did not believe. We are exhibiting the same nonchalant attitude to the warnings we receive, not from the televangelists, but from the everyday catastrophes we have been experiencing.

With all these catastrophes taking place in so many areas, why are televangelists not spending more time trying to arouse the consciousness of their audiences to the signs of the times, rather than focusing on the lack of financial support for the ministry? Why ridicule members of their congregation for their failure to pay tithes? Money seems to be the focal point of most televangelists' sermons.

On the Mount of Olives, after the disciples were amazed at the beauty and enormity of the stones of the buildings, Jesus cautioned them about the vulnerability of life (Mark 13:1–8). Jesus told them that there shall not be left one stone upon another. The curiosity of the disciples led them to ask more questions. They wanted to know when those things would take place and what sign could be expected for the fulfilment of the things of which Jesus spoke.

At that point, Jesus cautioned them to be careful and wary of deception, because there would be false prophets who would claim to be Christ. Jesus also told them that there would be wars and rumors of wars. He said they should not be troubled, because those things must come to pass but the end would not be yet. Nation would rise against nation and kingdom against kingdom, and there would be earthquakes in divers places, and there would be famines and troubles that would be the beginning of sorrows.

It has become quite easy for us to lose sight of the goal when there is so much distraction in the world. We tend to allow ourselves to be drawn in by the things that excite us, and to look away from the things that depress us. The world has gone through many changes since creation and is now in turmoil. Country rose up against country and wars were fought again and again over the centuries. First they were fought with swords and spears, and soldiers rode on horses. Then there were submarines and torpedoes. Now armies fly jets and fight with bombs, guns, guided missiles, and drones. These things can be very worrisome, but we must remember the words of Jesus: "These things must needs be, but the end shall not be yet."

We can well take comfort in these words, but we must also remember the parable of the ten virgins. It will serve us well to understand the significance of preparedness; we cannot afford to run out of oil, lest our lamps go out and we miss the arrival of the bridegroom.

People often believe that there is enough time to get ready. Jesus cautioned about the deception of time when He told the parable of the man who experienced great increase of his crops. The man decided that he would pull down his small barns and build greater ones in order to store his grain, saying, "I will relax and enjoy my grain for many years hence."

But Jesus said to him, "Thou fool this night thy soul is required of thee then to whom will these things belong?"

Most televangelists preach about the here and now, completely forgetting about the hereafter. They amass millions under the guise that they are using the money to help the needy and establish religious schools. There is a cliché that we would do well to think about: "We brought nothing into this world, and we can take nothing out."

Those of us who watch televangelists deliver their sermons on Sundays realize that preaching about eternal damnation is a thing of the past. Back then, preachers would remind us that the "wages of sin is death, but the gift of God is eternal life."

Anyone who has a little knowledge about finances and banking knows that the greater the principal, the greater the interest. Where there is no principal, there is no interest. A vast amount of money deposited into the bank can and will produce a generous amount of interest. Business is never conducted on a full-payment basis. A contract agreement allows the business an agreed period of time to complete payment. We should not allow ourselves to be fooled.

We should not allow ourselves to be distracted by preachers who tell us that God did not intend for us to be poor. "The Lord maketh poor and maketh rich: he bringeth low and lifteth up" (1 Sam. 2:7). We are told this because such preachers know that the wealthier we are, the more we can give to their organizations.

Jesus once said to his disciples, "The poor you have with you always, me you have not." When a disaster strikes, there is no time to think of whether we are rich or poor. The only thought that enters our minds is finding a way of escape. Whatever we do, the fact remains that riches mean nothing if we are not prepared to give account for the condition of our souls.

"The wilderness and the solitary place shall be glad for them; and the desert shall rejoice, and blossom as a rose" (Isa. 35:1). This prophecy was made by Isaiah sometime during the eighth century BC. Isaiah also foretold Christ's birth (7:14, 9:6), His deity (9:6–7), His ministry (9:1–2, 42:1–7, 61:1–2), His death (52:1–53:12) and His future millennial reign (chapters 2, 11, 65).

It is obvious that these things are already happening, which tells us that we are likely approaching or in the end time. Televangelists are filling the airways with glad tidings of great joy, peace on earth, and good will to all men. However, are they really interested in our spiritual well-being and our readiness to face the end time? Or are they interested in our ability to fulfill their financial needs? They sell books, but none of them explains Daniel's prophecy. They sell CDs, but none of them explains the Song of Solomon. They organize cruises, but none of them explains the plight of Jonah from the ship to the belly of the whale. They sell tickets for trips to the Holy Land, but they do not preach about Paul's missionary journey.

Why is money such a sought-after commodity by televangelists in a time when they should be concentrating on the words of Jesus?

The world is tottering on the brink of destruction, and its present situation is chaotic. Scientists are trying to prove or disprove the existence of God and the beginning of the world. There is racial and political unrest in the West, economic instability in Europe, civil war in the Middle East, and threats of war among the superpowers. Despite the signs and warnings, we are engulfed in our lives of earthly pleasures and stark disrespect for the Word of God. All the while, the televangelists seek to enhance the financial status of the church's pastor rather than the spiritual health of its members or reconciliation between God and sinful humanity.

CHAPTER 7

TELEVANGELISTS AND THE TITHE

Money has become the focal point of almost every sermon and every inspirational speech by televangelists. They say that once we trust God and make donations to their organizations, our lives will be changed for the better. God's favor will fall on us, and all our needs will be supplied by Him. Meanwhile, the televangelists expect us to supply their needs.

Again, I ask why money is such an important factor today when souls are lost in the turmoil of this world. Can a monetary value be placed on your soul? If so, how much would you give in exchange?

Our present civilization requires that we use money as legal tender; without it, we are unable to acquire the necessities of life. We understand that televangelists need money in order to keep their programs on the airways, and also to obtain, not the luxuries, but the necessities of life.

To say, however, that if we do not give a certain amount of money to the church, we are robbing God, as per Malachi

3:8, is misleading, since money was not the only factor in the prophet's accusation. This is set forth in Nehemiah 13:12–13, where we learn of the redistribution of the tithe of grain, new wine, and oil. In our time, we do not think of presenting commodities as part of the tithe. If we did, the televangelists, like the priests of the Old Testament, would have the responsibility of redistributing those offerings.

On any given Sunday, if we turn our television, we can find a preacher talking about nothing but prosperity. He'll talk not about heaven or hell, not about Christ dying on the cross to save sinners, but rather about the money needed to carry on his work of spreading the gospel.

While it may seem that I am criticizing all televangelists, not all are money grabbers. Some are sincere and honest about the Word of God, and even dare to preach about His saving grace and the price of redemption. They do not offer you prayer cloths or spring water or a promise that God will send you a financial windfall. They do not place their hands on congregants' foreheads and push them to the ground, claiming they are healed. They do not offer for sale a cross on a chain or a Scripture verse on a bookmark. Such props are always used for a specific purpose, and that purpose is to influence the viewing public to provide donations.

On the other hand, some of them create competition among the people to encourage them to exercise their talent as well as express their faith in God through song. There is such a program on BET called *Sunday Best*. In this competition, entrants sing a gospel song or hymn of their choice and are judged by a panel. The winner is awarded a contract to make gospel CDs, which may provide financial success as well as fame for that person.

These competitions are great for the contestants, but what are the benefits to the church, the evangelist who produces the show, the station that televises the show, or the companies that sponsor the show? As with everything else, money is involved. So I ask, who is reaping the benefits and for what is the money used?

Some religious organizations run primary schools and charge fees. Some have their own colleges and provide ample education to their students. It is questionable whether there is a tuition charge or not, but whatever the answer, money is involved in some form or other.

We hesitate to place these institutions under scrutiny, since we understand it takes money to run schools and colleges. But when an organization has 501(c)(3) tax-exempt status, tracking money flow becomes difficult. The organization cannot be required to be audited, which provides its accountants with some level of immunity against investigation.

I believe that poor people are being exploited by so-called ministers of the gospel who use the Word of God to enrich themselves. They prey upon the vulnerability of people whose faith in God exceeds the limitations of men. In other words, they present themselves as so holy, Spirit-filled, and in tune with God's will that it is almost impossible for them to be anything but righteous. They act as if they are the oracles of God, which gives them the authority to pass on to anyone the blessings they receive from God. The problem is that those blessings have a price tag attached.

Believe me, I am not anti-money, anti-wealth, or anti-prosperity. Wealth and prosperity have been around since Abraham, Isaac, and Jacob. The problem is the way evangelists obtain their wealth.

We know that Abraham's personal sacrifice and his faith in God resulted in his wealth. Isaac was the sacrifice Abraham offered to God in his spirit, not expecting to receive any special favors in return, but God saw his faithfulness and blessed him. Jesus was the sacrifice offered in the flesh by God as a special favor to redeem a lost world.

Jesus did not come to condemn the law and start a new ministry. He came to fulfill the law and perfect the ministry that was already in existence. He came to fulfill God's promise of reconciliation between Himself and fallen humanity.

Jesus's mission was completed, but humanity has not yet fully acknowledged or accepted the gift of redemption. While we may believe that the end time is near, we still find ourselves engrossed in the financial aspect of our lives—how much wealth we can accumulate and how much we can use that wealth to influence the decisions of those in authority. Those who have it know that wealth is power, and power provides control (Rev. 13:12–14). However, in the final analysis, we must think of the consequences we may suffer because of the decisions we make.

Corruption and violence in the earth were God's reasons for the destruction of all living creatures except for Noah and his family (Gen. 6:11–18). Despite the warnings of impending destruction, the people continued to live their lives of violence and corruption. They thought Noah was a fanatic because he had faith in Someone whom they did not know and probably did not care to know.

Are the televangelists of our time doing enough to warn the people of impending doom? Are they concentrating more on their financial health than on the spiritual health of the people? When they stand in the pulpit or behind the podium to preach, are they seeing a congregation of lost souls or are they seeing dollar signs? Are they trying to invite people to accept the offer of free salvation, or are they in the business of selling the truth? "Buy the truth, and sell *it* not; *also* wisdom, and instruction, and understanding" (Prov. 23:23). Televangelists would do well to think of this Scripture passage and study it before offering for sale anything purporting to be the truth from the Bible.

Jesus said, "I am the way, the truth and the life." I believe that any attempt to sell the truth is a repetition of the mistake that Judas made when he offered to betray Jesus for a mere thirty pieces of silver. Are the televangelists in the business of bringing the truth to those who need it, or are they just interested in fulfilling their own personal needs? We should not allow the televangelists to take us on a financial ride under the pretense of providing spiritual satisfaction. Any donations given should be made without the expectation of a return—whether in the form of a book, a CD, a ticket, or anything that appears to be an exchange.

In particular, we should avoid purchasing tickets to attend services in large convention centers or stadiums. If a televangelist is holding a service to promote his religious convictions and expand his audience, then why should he charge an admission fee? Should admission not be free?

Another thing we should find worrisome is the idea that televangelists are all promoting the same cause, yet they are divided in their beliefs and teachings. If evangelism is not a business, why are they engaged in competitive activities? Does it matter which denomination is responsible for the conversion of sinners? There are so many denominations, and each one of them strives to convince us that theirs is the right one, that they are the true followers of Christ. If they are all right and money is not the object, does it matter with which one we seek membership in? I suppose the choice is ours, but there is also a psychological element to their suggestions.

There is a preacher whom I admire. I watch him preach every Sunday morning on television.[7] He is a motivator and great inspirational speaker who knows how to grasp and hold his audience. He always begins his sermons with a joke, which relaxes the congregation. At the end of his service, he always says, "I never close without giving you the opportunity to make Jesus the Lord of your life. Will you pray this prayer with me?" He then says a short prayer, and

---

[7] Fox T.V channel 5

adds, "If you pray this simple prayer, I believe that you have become born again. Get into a Bible-based church and keep God into your lives."

This is where I believe that psychology comes into play. Once the prayer has been suggested and you have listened to his preaching, you feel an obligation to be part of his organization. The chances are high that you will become an active member or even a contributing partner financially.

I have commented previously on the size of these churches and the number of members they have. This particular church, with the pastor that I personally admire, is included in that scenario. The church occupies an old football stadium, which he purchased, renovated, and fitted out with Jumbotrons to facilitate the growing size of the membership. This building most likely was purchased through bank financing. All the visual effects had to be paid for, which called for the creation of a building fund. I believe that fund is duly supported by the church members and some business organizations. Sometimes funds are raised from book sales, cake sales, and ticket sales for special services.

Let me be clear. I am not trying to demonize this church or its pastor. All I want to do is make people aware of those who would use the Word of God to gain financial advantage by fleecing poor, unsuspecting congregations. While watching the services conducted by this influential speaker, I realized that the stadium is always packed to capacity. If each member of the audience gave two dollars, imagine the amount of money he would receive for one service. Multiply that by the number of services per month, and multiply again by the number of months in a year.

Televangelism is not only a business, it is a money-making machine. We know that whatever can be sold will be sold and whatever can be bought will be bought. Only those with the financial fortitude will have that privilege. But again I ask, can the truth be sold? "Buy the truth, and sell *it* not; *als*o wisdom, and instruction, and understanding" (Prov. 23:23).

CHAPTER 8

NEWS FLASH!

In an earlier chapter I said that televangelism is categorized as a not-for-profit business under section 501(c)(3) of the tax code. If there really is no profit in it, where does the money come from that televangelists use to purchase the luxurious cars, jets, and mansions that they own?

Case in point, recently a prominent television religious personality, Jan Crouch, passed. My sympathy and prayers go out to her family. When they announced her passing, they highlighted her financial holdings. They spoke about her many mansions and jets, but nothing about her evangelical organization.

An internet review stated that she was a cofounder of TBN, a religious network operating on national television. It said she owned a number of jets and thirteen mansions. This made me wonder, why would a televangelist need thirteen mansions and more than one jet? There may be an explanation, but will it be good enough?

I believe that some televangelists are genuine, but why are they not doing more to help the needy? When so many people have contributed to their organizations, is it fair that we should read about their many mansions, jets, cars, and whatever else they own? I am sure that many of the people contributing to these ministries do not own such things. They donate upon impulse, under the influence of preachers who tell them that they will receive a blessing if they pledge a thousand dollars—or, as the preachers call it, sow a thousand-dollar seed to the ministry.

From the following picture, you can well see where the thousand-dollar seeds are sown.

This picture is an example of the type of mansion allegedly owned by many of the televangelists. While I intend no disrespect to anyone, people should be aware of the commitment they are making when they listen to and watch televangelists.

As I have stated many times, not all televangelists are exploiting us. There are some who are definitely interested in their audiences' spiritual needs and well-being. We commend them for holding the truth sacred.

The object of this book is not to ridicule all televangelists, but to bring to the attention of believers in the Word of God the availability of free salvation. We do not have to pay for God's redemptive favor. We just must believe and repent of our sins. We do not have to sow a thousand-dollar seed. "Buy the truth, and sell *it* not; *also* wisdom, and instruction, and understanding" (Prov. 23:23 KJV).

With so many churches, religious organizations, and televangelists providing services on television and at stadiums, why is there still so much hatred and violence in the country? Is it because they are only preaching to the choir and not trying to effect love and change in the hearts of the people? Preachers seem to be more interested in tithes and offerings than in the spiritual, psychological, and physical condition of their listeners. In 2008 we witnessed the inauguration of a black president, and for the next eight years there was nothing but hatred among the races. Where is the caring? Where is the love? Where is the unity?

In 2011, when Mitt Romney was running against Barack Obama, Romney chose Paul Ryan as his running mate for the vice-presidential position. At every campaign stop, Paul Ryan would say, "We have to take our county back." Of course, this is political jargon. But my question to Paul Ryan is, who do you want to take the country back from, and how far back do you want to take it? To a time before slavery was abolished? Before the Martin Luther King era? Only Paul Ryan knows what he meant.

Mitt Romney is a professing Christian. So, the welfare of the people should have been his foremost concern. Romney lost, and Barack Obama was elected for his second term.

Then came 2016, and Donald Trump, who professed to be nothing other than a good businessperson, used similar jargon: "I will make America great again." What does the word "again" imply? Does this mean that America has not been great since blacks were given the right to vote? Or are we to understand that America was not great when it had a black president?

We will never know what is in the minds of Donald Trump and Paul Ryan. Putting all of this aside, the problem is that we need to return to the Bible. Proverbs 29:18 says, "Where there is no vision the people perish." We need leadership with a vision for the survival of the people. Leadership is not thrust upon the shoulders of government appointees, but rather upon all those who can influence others with lesser ability to choose a better way of life. Moses was not a government appointee. He was a man chosen by God to lead a vast number of people from a land of bondage imposed by the pharaohs of Egypt.

Moses was a ruler, a leader, and spiritual adviser. He was not voted for by humanity, but was appointed by God. He stood before the people and explained the commandments and laws of God. Imagine what would have happened to him after the Israelites were lost in the wilderness, had he been an elected official. Even so, he paid the ultimate price when he vented his frustration on them. He was not allowed to enter the Promised Land.

Some televangelists today concentrate on tithes and donations rather than their audiences' spiritual needs. I heard one televangelist recently make an offer: "I will give you two books explaining certain prophecies of the Bible if you donate one hundred dollars." If this is not a cloaked sale, then what is?

The world is in turmoil. Racial tensions and hatred are on the rise. Political leaders create distrust between their countries and people of other countries. Spiritual leaders strive for larger congregations, more beautiful homes, more expensive cars, more books sold, and larger bank accounts. Some use their television shows to criticize the government and its policies.

Their utmost goal should be to use their spiritual influence to change the mind-set of the people, especially in a time of frustration and anger. "Give unto Caesar the things that are Caesar's and unto God the things that are God's." Judas was paid thirty pieces of silver for the betrayal of Christ, who willingly gave His blood as a ransom for our sins.

Read Hebrews 9:11–24.

His blood is not for sale.

About the Author

Karl Grosvenor attended Mercy College and graduated with a bachelor of science degree in business administration, with honors.

He spent several years working at one of the largest banks in New York after receiving a school of banking certificate from the American Institute of Banking in New York.

Karl has a vast amount of knowledge in church dealings. He was very active in his church work as well as being an authorized preacher, vice president of the young people's society, and member of the church choir. He collaborated with his president to organize an all-night prayer meeting and, with his president, co-conducted a play that he wrote for the church's zone meetings. He speaks occasionally to church congregations

Printed in the United States
By Bookmasters